Patchwork Color

Written by Felicia Law
Illustrated by Paula Knight

Published by Mercury Junior

Sunflowers

The flowers lift their faces
They open one by one
The children lift their faces
To catch the golden sun

The flowers stretch their petals
To catch the warmth and light
The children stretch on tiptoe
To match the sunflowers' height

Green crocodile

Make way!

Step aside!

Run and hide!

Don't delay!

Here comes a

Jaw snapping

Claw trapping

Mean green crocodile!

Little worm

I told
The little worm
That my favorite color
Was pink

The worm agreed with me

I think!

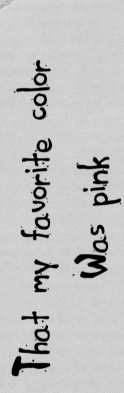

Blue waves

Sitting here

At the edge of the blue blue sea

There's just the blue blue blue sky

The blue blue birds

The blue blue waves

And me

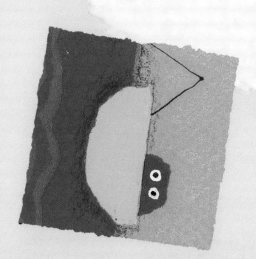

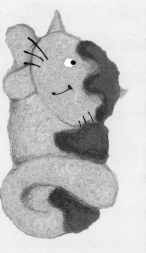

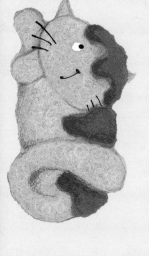

Ketchup

Just one little squeeze

And ketchup

Can fetch up

All over the place

All over the cat

All over the mat

All over the hat

Splat!

Purple paint

Red paints
Paint red

Blue paints
Paint blue

Mix them into purple
Purple paints

YOU!

Snowy day

Every time
I scrunched the crisp white snow
Into a ball
And let it go
Hitting the snowman
'Smack' on the nose
Where it melted in drips
And slowly froze

The snowman
Hit me back

Thwack!

The ball room

Plastic and yellow
Spongy like jello

I love bouncing

In the ball room

Slipping and flipping
Jumping and bumping
Stumbling and tumbling
Wriggling and giggling
Sliding and hiding
Flopping and toppling

I love bouncing

In the ball room

Oops!

Whoops!

Black

Stars that twinkle

Lights that show

Eyes that sparkle ·

· Bugs that glow

Tiny pinpoints ·

fade and grow

Even on the darkest night

A sky of black is full of light

This book introduces key words to your child

- ball
- bird
- black
- blue

- brown
- children
- crocodile
- eye

- face
- flower
- gold
- green

- sun
- sunflower
- wave
- white
- worm
- yellow

- purple
- red
- sea
- sky
- snow
- star

- light
- little
- orange
- paint
- petal
- pink

Mercury Junior
20 BLOOMSBURY STREET
LONDON WC1B 3JH

This edition published 2005 by
Mercury Books
20 Bloomsbury Street
London WC1B 3JH
ISBN 1-904668-80-1
Copyright © 2003 Allegra Publishing Ltd

Printed by D 2 Print Singapore